The Fundamentals
to Become a Successful
Store Manager

J. A. Thomas III

The Fundamentals to Become a Successful Store Manager. Copyright 2016. All rights reserved. Printed in the United States of America. No part of this book may be used or reproduced in any manner whatsoever without expressed written permission.

FIRST EDITION

ISBN 978-1523432462

Table of Contents

Introduction   iv

Part 1: You, the Manager

Your First Day	1
The Way You Look Matters	3
Act Like the Manager	4
Have a Positive Attitude	9
Your Office	12
Company Policy	14
The Customers	16
Profit	20
Goals	22
Time Management	26
Managing Tasks	30
Implement Systems	32
The Telephone	35
Security	37

Company Funds	42
Contests	44
A Foundation of Fundamentals	45
Payroll & Scheduling	47
Change is Coming	50
Think Outside the Box	52
Dealing With Stress	54
Ask for Help	56
Achieving Balance	58

Part 2 : Your Employees

Your Employees	62
Assistant Managers	64
Your Stories	66
Cell Phones	67
Clear Expectations	69
Listen	71
Praise in Public – Correct in Private	74

Show Appreciation	76
Motivation	77
Look for Changes	81
The Art of Training	83
Cross-training	87
Delegating With Follow-up	89
Relaying Information	93
Staff Meetings	95
Interviewing & Hiring	97
Performance Evaluations	101
Pay for Performance	103
Discipline	105
Corrective Action	108
Conflict Resolution	110
Termination	112
Turnover	113
Summary	116

Introduction

This is the most informative and easy to understand book you'll ever read on becoming an effective manager. This book combines decades of experience with multiple business operating systems to offer guidance on some basic management principles and procedures that have been around for a long time. To a successful manager, words like respect, delegation, discipline, teamwork and attitude are very important. You'll find this book very helpful, no matter what type of business you manage. Refer to this as a study guide for learning the people skills and best practices to perform your job better than ever before.

This book will also assist the men and women you meet every day who manage the hardware stores, fast food restaurants, auto parts stores, dry cleaners, clothing outlets and numerous other businesses. They're woven into the fabric of your life. When their staff performs well, you're happy. Your orders at the drive-through are right the first time. The car battery you bought fits and works perfectly. The cashier properly bagged all of your groceries and put them in your cart. She didn't even forget to add the double-bagged chicken she set off to the side.

The employees were cheerful, attentive and thanked you for your business. Customers really like going there and come back often. When that happens, thank the manager. His or her direction, dedication, training, hard work and complete knowledge of the business paid off with you, the satisfied customer.

Unfortunately, this isn't always the case. You asked for no mayo and two orders of onion rings, not double mayo and no onion rings. You told the man you wanted a battery for a 2010 Ford Fusion, but it doesn't even fit in the tray. Now you have to drive all the way back to the auto parts store and deal with those people who can't look up the correct part.

Does this sound familiar? Well, that's the manager's responsibility, as well. He or she didn't train the employees to properly serve the customers. Instead, the manager was in the office, struggling over the work schedule, and didn't even know there was a problem. *Who's in charge here?* you wonder. *Who promoted this person? This company is terrible! I will never shop here again!*

The sad fact is that it's probably not the manager's fault. Someone put the most productive and dedicated employee in charge with little or no training. No one covered time management, training, follow up or goal-setting. The stork never showed up with the miracle of competent management.

The simple truth is most people know a great deal about what it takes to be promoted to store manager and very little about what it takes to stay there. Their orders at the drive-through were always right. The battery always fit the first time. They always showed up to work on time and took pride in whatever they did. They were talented, well liked and respected. How did something so right go so wrong? Keep reading.

This book is divided into two parts. Part 1 is **You, the Manager**. We'll cover a few things you need to face the challenges and rewards ahead. Part 2 is **Your Employees**. All of your knowledge and skills need to be taught to your employees so the end result is serving satisfied customers and running a profitable business.

A notes section has been provided at the end of this book to write down areas you want to remember or particular management skills you might need to improve.

Part 1

You,

The Manager

*

Be where the action is as often as you can. Learn your customers' names and make sure they know yours.

*

Your First Day

Your first day as manager is truly an exciting time. In the beginning, it almost seems hard to keep your thoughts straight. There's so much to do and learn. To top everything off, you're a little nervous, as well. Being nervous is a good thing! That means you have a grasp of your new level of responsibility and want to perform well.

The first piece of advice is to take it easy. Handle this new level of authority with dignity and class. Your employees already know you're the new manager, so you don't have to prove it. Don't begin your manager career by charging in with your guns blazing and correcting everything you see wrong. You'll make a terrible first impression if you begin by announcing that everything is going to change because a new dictator has been appointed and he is to be feared. Your goal should be to earn the employees' respect and trust so they'll follow you willingly.

Get to know your employees and allow them to get to know you. Meet everyone and learn their names. Find out what you can about their likes and dislikes. Pay attention to those who work hard, while noting those who are on their cell phones all day.

You should check to make sure everyone reports to work on time. Watch, listen and learn so you can begin to piece together the required knowledge to lead your staff effectively.

Look around and take some notes. Learn how the store was run before you took over. Some areas might be operating perfectly and your job is to maintain that level. Other areas may be lacking expertise or efficiency and will require your guidance to improve the situation.

In the beginning, your job is to be the learner. Gathering this information will assist you in formulating a plan to begin your management journey. You have to begin somewhere, and that requires a plan. It's usually best to make your first few days uneventful. You'll have plenty of opportunities to put all of your managerial skills into action, but the time for that is not on your first day.

The Way You Look Matters

There's one part of being a manager that everyone sees. It's with you every minute. You can't hide from it or pretend it doesn't exist. It speaks volumes without you ever saying a word. Everyone will have an opinion about it. What is it? It's how you look and dress.

Why is your appearance so important, and who really cares? Everyone does because it makes a statement. It sets an example. Dressing the part of a manager says you take pride in your responsibilities and you carry yourself as the leader. When you come in contact with your employees and your customers, you look professional.

Gone are the days of showing up wearing dirty tennis shoes or that belt you should've burned two years ago. That look of the unshaven and rugged Miami Vice detective is history. Coming to work in flip-flops and cut-off jeans on your day off isn't a good idea. Either paint your fingernails or don't. You didn't fight your way through a hostile jungle to get to work, so don't look like you did. When you get a pay raise, reinvest a small part of it to upgrade your appearance. Be neat, clean and well-dressed to portray this new and important role.

Act Like the Manager

Once you've been promoted to manager, your future looks bright. The hard work and dedication have paid off. You stand a little straighter and you smile a little bigger. Your company has put the ultimate measure of faith in you to lead employees and operate a successful business.

A certain level of prestige accompanies the title of "store manager." It usually comes with a salary increase and your own office, which you get to make uniquely yours. From that point on, you get to introduce yourself to the customers as the manager. Family and friends have probably congratulated you on your achievement. You have finally arrived!

The trouble is, along with this new title comes an awesome responsibility, and unless you have previous management experience, you've never done this job before. You've performed various employee duties and worked for a manager or two, but you've never actually been a manager.

This is where you must transform from an employee or assistant manager to the person who must act like the manager and conduct yourself accordingly.

Employees don't respect the position; they respect the person. Someone is always watching everything you say and do. This is part of becoming a leader, so always bear this in mind before you speak or act.

There's nothing wrong with expecting results from your employees and being firm about their individual responsibilities. Your job isn't to be popular. It's to operate a profitable business through hard-working employees who do it because they respect you. The manager is measured by results, and those expectations of results should be passed on to the employees.

Take full responsibility for your requests. Don't ever blame your supervisor or the company for instructions you give your employees to carry out. You'll give the impression of being weak and not a team player. The buck stops with you. Setting a five o'clock deadline means just that. Assigning a $10,000 sales quota means $9,000 won't be acceptable. The company has issued the proper direction, and has entrusted you to achieve it. That will never happen if you don't set employee standards of performance every day. Be fair, but firm.

Never use profanity with your employees. It doesn't make you cool or accentuate a point. The employees won't jump any higher or work any harder because you believe the use of profanity demonstrates you really mean it this time. If it's been a habit for you, then break it. Surely, by practicing a little self-control, you can learn how to make a request or give feedback using all the other words in your vocabulary.

Maintain your composure in your daily interactions with the staff. Things will go wrong every day, but that doesn't give you an excuse to lose your cool or raise your voice. When that happens, you lose control of yourself, the employees and the business. Remember, if everything always operated smoothly, your company wouldn't need a manager. Stay calm so you can stay in charge.

Fraternizing with your employees is a death sentence for you ever becoming an effective manager. It may not seem like a big deal to grab a hamburger with Shirley after work or join Mike's bowling team on Saturdays, but those simple things will undermine everything you're trying to achieve. In everyone's mind, you've made friends with some of the staff.

The ones who don't bowl or dine with you will feel like those who do are receiving special treatment. The employees you do spend personal time with will wonder how you can discipline them for being late to work when you have plans with them that weekend. Fraternizing with or, even worse, dating your employees means you may as well start looking for a new job.

Don't act or speak in any way that someone could even remotely construe as sexual in nature. Stay out of conversations regarding a person's sexual orientation. Lewd jokes or gestures make most people feel uncomfortable. Physical contact other than a handshake or a pat on the back is usually not a good idea. Lawsuits will arise out of perceived sexual harassment by a manager, so be careful what you do and say.

Discrimination is also a serious offense. Comments about race, religion, sex, physical disabilities or any other area where you might imply that one type of person will usually perform better or worse than another is against the law and has no business in the workplace. Every employee has the right to expect you to judge his or her work solely on job performance, not any prejudices or stereotypes you might have.

Finally, the issue of social media. A moment's loss of your common sense will come back to bite you. Think before you post anything for everyone to see. You're the manager of your store now. If you don't want your mother and your supervisor to read it, then don't post it.

While the store manager position is loaded with rewards, it's also full of responsibilities and pitfalls. Don't be one of those managers who's sorry after the fact. Set the proper example. Follow company guidelines and insist your employees do the same. Treat your employees equally and with respect. Teach them how to become successful and help them when they need it. The day you master these fundamentals regularly in your store, the sky is the limit for you.

Have a Positive Attitude

There are almost not enough words in the English language to describe the difference between someone with a positive attitude and someone with a negative attitude. The overall contrast in results can be mind-boggling. Someone who dresses the part of a manager but has a negative attitude will never become successful. So why does one person have such a positive attitude while another can't find anything positive even to think? Henry Ford once said "Whether you think you can or you think you can't – you're right."

Your attitude is the result of what you **choose** to think about. Those thoughts govern your actions and interactions during the course of the day. No one can give you a positive or negative attitude. You make that decision. Good and bad things happen to most managers every day. The difference lies in the way you react to various situations. You can view your glass as either half full or half empty – the choice is yours.

Having a positive mental attitude is an all-the-time thing. It generates increased energy levels and higher productivity. Positive managers believe in themselves and their employees, while refusing to let any obstacles get in the way of getting the job accomplished. They look for good work from the employees and respond with positive feedback and encouragement. This positive attitude creates an overall upbeat and exciting atmosphere that rubs off on everyone in the workplace. When a customer walks into a dress shop, for example, she can tell what kind of manager operates it by the way the employees serve her. Are they friendly, courteous and upbeat? If the answer is yes, then so is the manager.

Managers with a negative attitude, however, also transfer that attitude to their employees, and every one of them will mirror it. There's no such thing as employees having a great day and feeling good about their jobs when the store manager came to work with a negative attitude. No one wants to work for, or be around, someone who's negative all the time.

Leave personal problems outside the walls of your business. When you enter your store, make the choice to focus on the job. At times this can be difficult, but you have to remember your employees watch you and will mirror your attitude. Taking the day off to handle the situation would be better than bringing a bad attitude to work.

The manager has to notice, and act upon, employee inefficiency and mistakes. That doesn't mean, however, these are the only areas of importance. Falling into the rut of noticing only the bad in everything will lead to an overall negative attitude from everyone in your store. Always try to find more positive than negative in your daily interactions with employees. Make the choice to be that positive leader your employees will follow, so that together you can achieve the goals you've set out to accomplish.

Your Office

In Greek mythology, Mount Olympus was the home of the gods, the most powerful and all-knowing rulers in the universe. From that high point, they could oversee the everyday lives of mortal humans and exercise their powers however they saw fit.

Although your office may have your name on the door, it's not Mount Olympus. You don't want to take up permanent residence there. While many important functions like interviewing, scheduling and money handling all require the privacy and security of your office, you don't want to be one of those managers who always finds 9,000 reasons to be in it. That type of manager always needs to shuffle some kind of paper in there or perform those secret and mysterious manager tasks that require closing the office door, and virtually sealing him- or herself off from the business, the employees and the customers.

Be where the action is as often as you can. Learn your customers' names and make sure they know yours. Tell Tracy what a great job she is doing. Make sure Tony doesn't forget to front the end caps again.

Training, motivation and all the other responsibilities that come with this job happen "out there," not locked in a twenty square-foot room with your name on it. Always remember the name plate is changeable.

Company Policy

The policies within your company are the result of years of refining the principles and best practices that form the foundation of your business. These are non-negotiable rules and regulations that all employees and managers must strictly adhere to in order to ensure employee safety, make sure everyone is treated fairly and help mold the image the company is seeking. They also teach employees and managers alike how to serve the best possible product to the customers, and ultimately make a profit.

Upholding and enforcing company policies requires understanding every last detail about those policies yourself. Become familiar with the policy manual and ask your supervisor to explain any points you find unclear. Your job is to set the proper example without exception.

Personally review the employee manual with every new hire so all your employees will understand every aspect of the company expectations regarding conduct and performance. You can't hold an employee accountable for policy violations if you didn't clearly explain the company's position in detail.

Being promoted to the store manager doesn't give you a free ticket to circumvent or ignore company policies. Being in a hurry or serving several customers at once is no excuse to take shortcuts. These rules apply to everyone, every day. If you bent the rules in the past, you must stop bending them now that you're the manager.

Every time you ignore a policy or break a company rule, your employees will take notice. If you give the impression the rules don't matter, your employees will emulate your behavior. They'll be doing their own thing in their own way, without any regard for the regulations in place. The day that happens, any manager will be in big trouble. Company policy begins with you demonstrating compliance by example. By doing this, you can effectively expect the same from your employees.

The Customers

Customers are the life blood of any company. They pay all your expenses and produce all your profits. They make it possible for you and millions of other employees to have a job. Every dress or drill you sell has one goal – make your customers happy with your business so they want to return.

Everyone in your store should understand the importance of serving each customer at a higher level than the competition does. The products and services you offer should not only satisfy the customer's needs, they should also exceed his or her expectations. Customers can choose where to shop. If they're not completely satisfied with the products and services you offer, they'll take their business elsewhere. Pretend every customer entering your business wears a badge that reads, "Treat me well, because I don't ever have to come back."

Do you turn cartwheels and phone home every time you order a chili dog with fries and the store actually served it hot, in a bag, with napkins? The answer is no. You made a deal with the business to pay money in exchange for a chili dog with fries, served hot and in a timely fashion.

You never promised to come back or advise any of your friends to eat there. The restaurants that serve your food the way you order it (or not) can make you want to come back or not want to come back. The ball's in their court.

Simply supplying what's on the road sign, even if it's done perfectly, isn't necessarily good customer service. You might as well say, "What do you want?" "Here it is." "Give me the money." Business is a myriad of facts, figures, procedures and statistics. Dealing with customers, however, is much more personal.

Offering superior customer service begins with the hiring process. If an employee simply doesn't care, that attitude will show every day and with every customer. Having employees with a bad attitude is a deadly poison no business can long survive. Hire employees with a friendly disposition and basic manners. If they don't have that when you hire them, you won't be able to teach them.

Seemingly prehistoric words like "please," "thank you," "yes ma'am" and "no sir" go a long way in demonstrating basic respect and making customers feel special when they bring their needs to your business. This starts with the manager and filters down to every employee.

In addition to offering what the road sign says, it's most often the little things that will separate your store from the competition and provide your customers with a positive, memorable shopping experience. Say "Good morning," instead of "Can I help you?" Open the door for your customers. Offer to carry their trays or take the bags to their cars. Introduce yourself and ask their name. Now, she's not only a customer; she's Mary Wright. Compliment a dress or a car. Tell Roy what a well-mannered son he's raising. What a difference it would make to say "Are you losing weight, Mr. Watkins?" Now you have a special business where customers like to shop and enjoy the individual attention they receive.

Learn this one early. The customers are always right. Even if you're right and they're dead wrong, they're still right. Winning the battle isn't worth losing the war. When a customer has a problem, the manager has a problem. If the person is upset or even irate, remain calm and try to put yourself in the customer's shoes. Remember, driving all the way back to your store because your staff didn't do something properly is no fun and a waste of everyone's time.

This is the time to shine. Learn the words **"You're right, Mr. Customer**." "I would be upset too." "I apologize for the inconvenience." "What can I do to make this right?"

Exceed the customer's request, if at all possible. He or she will become a customer for life and tell everyone else to do business with you. If the customer wants the oil change for half price, give it to him or her at no charge, if your company allows. If they won't take a refund, then offer two coupons for a free service or product on their next visit. Do something, anything, to retain this customer's business. Everyone works too hard to bring customers in the door to let them get away for life just because Jenny neglected to ring up the curtain rods at the register because she didn't check the bottom of the shopping cart.

It sounds so simple. Treat the customers the way you want to be treated. Make them feel special and their business appreciated. Set the example as the manager. Do everything in your power to make this happen in your store every day and insist every employee do the same. Customers will notice, and they'll be back.

Profit

Every customer waited on, every gallon of paint sold and every oil change performed is designed for one purpose - to make a profit. It's the reason there's a manager with employees in a building with the lights turned on. Profit pays for that. If the business doesn't make a profit over time, either there'll be no more business to run, or a new manager will be chosen in an attempt to make a profit. None of this is personal. It's strictly business.

Did you ever drive past a business that had recently closed and ask yourself, "Why?" Every time you visited the store, it was always busy. The answer is almost always the same. The business didn't make a profit.

Conducting a lot of business is not necessarily making a profit. There are two types of profit: **gross profit** and **net profit**. If you sell a hammer for $5 and it costs you $3, you just made $2 in gross profit. But even if you sell 500 hammers this month, you still need to sell a whole lot more just to break even in the business. Rent, the electric bill, payroll and more all come due each month.

So even though a lot of money is changing hands, it's possible to not make any net profit. That's what's left after all the expenses are paid. The evidence of this is all around you every day with the closed businesses in your city.

You need to understand this simple truth. This is why you are given payroll limits, spending limits and sales goals. These limits are all designed to control expenses while achieving your sales goal to make a net profit. Many times, the difference between a store making a profit or suffering a loss falls squarely on the store manager's shoulders.

The manager's attention to these details is of paramount importance to make a net profit. Every light that doesn't need to be on, every dime of inventory that comes up missing and every hour an employee wastes cuts into net profit. Keep a watchful eye and do your part to make your business a profitable one.

Goals

If you were to ask most people whether they have goals, they would tell you they do. If you were to dig a little deeper, however, you would find they're nothing more than a collection of wants and wishes. So what constitutes a true goal? What makes you keep your eyes on the prize and really try to achieve it every day? Why is having a goal even necessary in the first place?

Everyone has small goals, whether they realize it or not. Arriving at work on time or having dinner prepared by 7 p.m. are small daily goals you perform without really giving them much thought. People really do understand goals and how to achieve them. So what's the problem? Why doesn't that understanding translate into setting and achieving goals for the business?

You find it easy to remember and act upon daily goals because you're constantly reminded of them. Your watch tells you if you made it to work on time, and your final destination was clear. The clock on the wall says 7 p.m., and a group of hungry people are gathered around the dinner table, so serving food seems to be the right thing to do.

What you see and hear, as well as the people around you, all serve as reminders to perform a certain task, in a certain way, by a certain time. The goal was clear, attainable and achieved.

Setting business goals is crucial to achieving success. They set the desired result and serve as a report card for the manager and the staff. The trouble is without reminders, the goals aren't always so obvious. Your store can serve a lot of customers and still make no profit. The floors can be spotless, but your business doesn't make enough money to survive. So where do you start, and what do you do? Where's that daily reminder of how the store stands in relation to the goal everyone set out to achieve?

The first step is to set the goal. It should be attainable, but not so easy that it can be reached with minimal effort. Just because your store has been achieving $10,000 a week in sales, doesn't mean it's not capable of doing twice that. So why not try what's never been done? Who says it will never happen, if you've never tried? Vince Lombardi, the legendary coach of the Green Bay Packers, once said, "Perfection is impossible. But if we chase it, we can catch excellence."

Your supervisor might issue your store a goal each month, but that's just a starting point. What's your goal, and what's the plan to make it happen? Wishing you had a million dollars is one thing. Setting a goal to make a million dollars and implementing a plan to make it happen is something entirely different. Keep setting higher goals and reaching for more. You might amaze yourself at what you can achieve if you set a goal, work hard to achieve it and don't let any obstacles get in your way.

Write down your goals in the weekly planner. Now it's not a want or a wish- it's a goal. Every day when you review your weekly planner, it stares right back at you. The minute you wrote down that goal, it became yours.

In order to be effective, the entire staff needs to understand the goal, as well, and be reminded of it. Now it becomes a part of daily business and is firmly entrenched in the culture of your store.

Implement a system, to serve as a daily reminder for every employee to understand those important, and ever-present, goals. You could simply place a monthly dry erase board next to the time clock. The green number is the goal, and the red number is the actual result.

Maybe handing out a daily notice works more effectively. Whatever the case, let the employees know with a written update listing the goal and the actual result. Your store either achieved it or it didn't, and everyone knows.

When you start setting goals and constantly trying to reach new heights in your business, this process will spill over into your personal life and the lives of your employees. The attitude and discipline required to achieve goals will become an all-the-time thing. You'll want more of that winning feeling.

So set the goals, write them down and keep your employees informed. When you achieve them, there will be a sense of satisfaction in knowing that together everyone accomplished what they set out to do. That's a good feeling.

Time Management

Time is a valuable commodity. There's just so much of it each day and then it's gone. Every customer served, every order pulled or every tire changed uses it. Once an hour has been wasted, it can never be regained. Whatever you could have accomplished in that hour, you now have to perform at some time in the future. This leads to the domino effect of continued diminished productivity. The more time you waste, the more work you'll have to do in the future. The old saying, "Never put off until tomorrow what you can do today," is never truer than with a manager who's in charge of getting the most out of everyone's time.

An eight-hour day has just 480 minutes. A five-day work week, then, has only 2,400 minutes. That hardly seems like enough time to accomplish an entire week's worth of work. There are customers to serve, training to be conducted, inventory to be stocked and so on. Carefully planning each week is your only hope of pulling it all together.

The simplest and most effective way of managing time and tasks is to utilize some type of weekly planning tool with a computer program or a planner book. It will help you keep up with vacation requests, employee anniversary dates, holidays and much more. That way your planner assists with making the work schedule, as well.

Lay out next week's plan toward the end of the present week. Include store goals, training, tasks and special projects. The staff meeting is Monday at 9 a.m. and should last an hour. The two new hires will train Tuesday and Wednesday from noon until 4 p.m. The store needs to exceed $25,000 next week to achieve budget. Tim will paint the restroom on Thursday and Friday from 6 p.m. until closing. This method of managing time will achieve the maximum results and go a long way toward accomplishing the greatest number of projects in the least amount of time.

You can't possibly include every daily task in a weekly planner, but time management still needs to be a part of accomplishing them. Set time limits on as many duties as possible (i.e., the parking lot should be swept in 30 minutes, and the stock needs to be put away by 4 p.m.).

These time limits will create a sense of urgency and accountability, so your employees will accomplish the tasks in the least amount of time. If you don't know how long a task should take, do it yourself to find out. Not setting time limits will almost certainly guarantee a ton of wasted time every day. Payroll dollars are called a "controllable" business cost for a reason.

This type of managing also gives you the opportunity to provide immediate feedback to your employees. You might say, "Tim, please restock the soda display in the next half hour, and check back with me when you're finished." Now Tim knows exactly how long you expect the job to take, and you'll get yet another opportunity to inspect his work and say, "Thanks, Tim." "That looks great." You told Tim exactly what you expected, and he did exactly what you wanted, so you noticed and thanked him. Wow! There's a manager people would love to work for.

A manager can't expect every employee to work every minute. It'll never happen. If any manager actually achieved that, then he or she wouldn't be with the company very long, because some large corporation would hire away this person to accomplish the impossible with its employees.

So manage everyone's time with reasonable expectations. There's no magic watch to stop and start time. Your job is to plan and manage it as best you can. Always remember that time is money, so spend it wisely.

Managing Tasks

Oh, the tasks to be accomplished when you're the manager. The store has to be open every day by 9 a.m. There's merchandise to be stocked, and all that daily paperwork. The floor guys come every Thursday night, and you personally inspect every pastry in this bakery to make sure it's perfect before it's sold. Just when you thought you were caught up and could take a breath, you learned that you have to tear down and send back the entire fishing lure display by Wednesday because the company has changed brands.

The constant and never-ending daily work the manager has to oversee to make sure the employees complete it properly and on time to keep the business running smoothly can be overwhelming, to say the least. If you're not mindful of this, your entire management existence will be to move from one task to the next all day long, and that's all. Simply completing tasks doesn't make you a good manager.

The sales are down 4% over the same period last year, the assistant manager is still having trouble making a work schedule and the night-time bartender needs more training on specialty drinks. These are the important areas that require your expertise.

Your employees and your business need some help, but they're not going to get it if your entire day consists only of making sure the floors are shiny and the aisles are well-stocked. Instead, make sure your assistant manager gets promoted and train a new employee to perform at a high level after only two weeks on the job. Time management, delegation, training and having efficient systems in place all play a critical role in helping you get past accomplishing the tasks, so you can spend the necessary time focusing on the direction of the business and training the employees to help you achieve it.

Getting stuck in the "tasks" is an easy trap to fall into. Take the time to look around. What do you see? There are displays, computers, paperwork, inventory and a hundred other things, all requiring your attention. But is that all you want to manage? The answer should be no. You want to manage a successful business. The trick is to handle the tasks as efficiently as possible, using everyone at your disposal, and move on to being the manager of the employees who help you serve your customers better than anyone else in your city.

Implement Systems

Efficient systems are important because they save time and money. You need to understand that most everything done in your store is actually a series of steps or processes required to complete a task. Systems answer the who, what, where, when, and how of everything from stocking the shelves to taking out the trash. When properly implemented, these systems don't require the manager to be involved every step of the way. The employees may change, but a good system endures.

If a light bulb burns out, whose job is it to replace it? A burned-out light bulb is no big deal until you find yourself working in the dark. If the manager notices it before anyone else does, and has to ask an employee to replace it, a system is needed. Assign checking, replacing and stocking light bulbs to an employee. In fact, make a duty list, and assign all daily, weekly or monthly duties to the staff. Now you have a system that works and saves time.

Some systems may already be in place, but after your inspection, you may find ways of improving them. Maybe one day you decide to watch your employee hose the parking lot.

Larry's Muffler Shop has been at this location since 1986, and you know the parking lot gets hosed every morning. At first glance, it may appear that no change is needed here. After all, it's just a hose and a parking lot. Simple. So why should we look for a better system?

Molly clocks in to work and walks out to the storage shed at the back of the parking lot to get the hose. She brings it over to the building, untangles it and hooks it to the faucet. When it's turned on, you notice it leaks from both the nozzle and a duct tape repair halfway down the hose, because sometimes cars run over it and cause a leak. She uses a small high-pressure nozzle because it makes it easier to wash the cigarette butts across the lot to the storm drain. You also notice she stops from time to time to shake the hose and work out the kinks. When she's finished, she takes the hose back to the shed and locks it up. The total time to complete her task with the present system is one hour.

Here's what you should have seen. If the hose is used every day, it shouldn't be locked up so far away from the building. Keep it inside and you'll save her the unnecessary trek all the way back to the shed. Next, purchase a heavier grade hose to withstand cars running over it and a hose reel so she can easily wheel it in and out.

Buy a new wide spray nozzle that will save time and water, because you now know your employees should sweep the parking lot before they hose it. That way, 78 gallons of water aren't used to push cigarette butts across the lot. You also need more ash trays outside to cut down on littering. The total time required to complete the job with this new system is only 30 minutes.

Your next thought may be, *Big deal. We only saved 30 minutes*. But that 30 minutes saved translates to $1,131 in payroll saved this year and every year! That doesn't include the hundred or so dollars in wasted water, and all this was accomplished by simply watching an employee hose the parking lot and looking for a better way to accomplish that simple task.

Don't walk around in a mindless maze of doing things a certain way because that's the way they've always been done. Take the time to really pay attention to everything that happens in your store. You might be amazed at what you learn and how much time and money you can save by implementing better systems. Would a larger cart help the stock get put away more quickly? Could you order store supplies monthly instead of weekly? Your net profits and days off will be so much better when efficient systems are all in place to get the job done.

The Telephone

You couldn't possibly be any busier today. Customers have been filing in since you opened the doors. Your employees don't have a second to spare. Everyone is working hard and giving excellent service, just like you trained them. On days like these, just catching your breath is a chore.

Then it happens. That ring. It always seems to happen at the worst possible time. Now you or one of your employees must stop this instant and handle it. The sound is, of course, the telephone.

The call could be for anything. "What time do you close?" "What's your special today?" "Are you hiring?" Many times, it's a potential or present customer needing some type of information about your business. That sounds pretty important.

Over the next few seconds, though, you can make it perfectly clear that this call was an unwelcome and unexpected interruption to your already busy day. You don't sound friendly because you don't feel friendly. The answers you give are short, and it's clear you don't want to be on the phone. So you end the call as quickly as possible, so you can get back to running your business and serving your customers. Doesn't something sound wrong here?

What you obviously should do is take the time to give the person on the other end of the line your undivided attention. Actually listen, and be as helpful as you can. You should sound friendly and professional. Realize the tone of your voice matters. It's not what you say, but the way you say it. Teach every employee to understand the importance of this opportunity. Always thank every customer for calling, because thankful is how you should feel when they call your business instead of your competitor down the street.

Security

Whether you manage an auto repair shop or a clothing store in the mall, you're responsible for company assets. Your employees are an asset, but you're also responsible for the safekeeping and proper use of tools, inventory, supplies, fixtures and, many times, cold hard cash. Trust plays no part in business security. All company assets should be verified, monitored and protected.

Placing merchandise and money well within the reach of employees and customers can tempt someone to steal from your company. The manager's job is to reduce or eliminate the opportunities that would allow people to take what they shouldn't and place the company's assets at risk. These losses leave fewer profits for upgrades, expansion and employee salary increases.

When assets are missing that didn't go through the normal business channels, like the cashier ringing them up, it's called **shrinkage**. The items are gone for good. When this happens, taking an inventory count or auditing the cash handling will usually reveal the discrepancies.

The two types of shrinkage are **internal** and **external**. Internal shrinkage occurs through employee neglect or dishonesty. External shrinkage is just what the name implies. It's when someone the business doesn't employ steals or makes a mistake. Shoplifting, unpaid customer bills or incorrect billing from vendors on shipments all contribute to external shrinkage.

If the cashier misses ringing up two bath towels at the register, and out the door they go, that's internal shrinkage. If a cook sneaks a ham out of the freezer to take home, that's internal shrinkage, as well. Studies reveal that for most businesses, internal shrinkage outweighs external shrinkage. Don't be naïve. It exists, and the manager has to prevent it. Some employees may feel that since your company is a large and profitable business, one little missing item here or there won't hurt anyone. The trouble is, when a lot of employees and customers share this mentality, the business is being devoured by a school of piranhas. It won't be operational very long.

There are several steps the manager can take to limit the opportunity for internal shrinkage. One is to keep the back and side doors locked at all times.

Managers are in charge of the keys, so they can oversee everything going out and coming in those doors. Placing merchandise in the bottom of the trash before it goes out, only to be retrieved later from the dumpster, is an old trick. When a shipment arrives, check it in to make sure all of it gets inside.

Make sure there's a clear policy in the employee manual regarding reentering the building after hours. Having three or more sets of keys out there can be a real temptation for someone. Alarm companies will typically offer a free monthly report on the opening and closing times, so arrange a copy to be sent once a month. Make the other managers aware that you monitor this, and no deviation should occur. Your job shouldn't be to catch someone in the act. It should be to stop any violations from happening in the first place.

There are also several ways to lose money at the cash register. A cashier could simply take money in small amounts, for example. Unfortunately, a lunch here and a drink there add up over time. The money count will obviously be wrong at the end of the shift. Address the problem immediately by holding the employee accountable so it stops in the beginning. If it doesn't, you need a new cashier.

The cashier could also give the customer the appearance of ringing up all the merchandise on the register to get the total, only to void the transaction while still accepting payment. In this case, the cashier would keep the entire amount of that sale. There will be no receipt, of course, so the manager always needs to check voided transactions for authenticity.

Falsified refunds account for shrinkage, as well. The cashier writes or rings up fictitious merchandise for a refund and pockets the money. All refunds should be monitored at the end of every shift to prevent this.

External shrinkage through shoplifting can also be a killer. Although most businesses use mirrors and cameras to deter this type of loss, nothing replaces good old-fashioned training to teach the employees to notice, and act upon, any type of suspicious behavior they see from the customers.

A group of people who enter the store and immediately separate should attract your attention. Someone wearing excessive clothing for the weather could mean paying for merchandise was never in the plan.

Customers who constantly look around to check who's watching are usually signaling they're up to no good. It's sad, but it's the reality of running a business.

Have some system in place so an employee can alert other employees to keep an eye out when anyone notices suspicious behavior. It could be announcing a code or secret word over the loudspeaker. The point is you have to do something.

Another example of external shrinkage is your store's incoming shipments. Check in the orders thoroughly every single time. The store manager is responsible for making sure the store actually receives everything it's billed for. Carelessness in this area can be very costly.

The need for security will never diminish. Any way you can conceive to get around the systems or rules that allow any employee or customer to benefit at the expense of your company, someone else has already thought of. You are the manager of a store filled with temptation. Pay attention to details and protect the assets because everyone will benefit.

Company Funds

Your company's policies and procedures to handle cash and make bank deposits are a very serious matter. Never deviate from these guidelines. They've been set up to ensure the safety of company funds and the employees. Your utmost attention to detail is required each and every time you handle the proceeds from the business. Leaving the safe unlocked, miscounting money or forgetting to make the bank deposit is a level of carelessness most companies won't tolerate.

Properly counting money and making change for a sales transaction are not skills the average human is born with. All employees need to be trained to perform them perfectly. Every dime of money that moves should be counted at least twice. The cashier first counts the change when removing it from the register, and then counts it aloud when it's given to the customer. The manager counts the money after every shift, and then recounts it to ensure accuracy. Then it's locked in the safe until a deposit is made.

Get the daily deposits to the bank on time and without exception. Making them during the day usually works the best for safety reasons. Take precautions so it's not obvious you're carrying a large sum of cash. Carry it in something with no bank markings. If thieves will snatch purses, they'll definitely go for a bank bag if they know you have one, so be safe.

Cash registers are an obvious target in your store. Leaving large sums of cash in plain view to flash in front of customers every time the register opens is begging for a robbery. Keep enough change in the register to conduct business properly, and periodically remove the overage to put in the safe.

Company funds are not your personal lending institution. Borrowing $10 or $20 until payday might not seem like a big deal until an unexpected audit occurs and the truth comes out. Don't jeopardize your career over something that should never happen.

Keep in mind that all the cash you're in charge of pays for next week's stock order, hiring another cashier for second shift and the raise you're hoping for next month. All that sounds pretty important, so treat it accordingly.

Contests

Store contests can turn an average month into an exciting one. They're designed to increase sales and profits by creating an atmosphere of competition and increased productivity.

If your company sponsors contests, then it becomes your job to promote them. Don't just pin the notice to the bulletin board and forget it. Kick it off with enthusiasm. Explain the goals, rules and prizes. Get your employees to make a commitment to participate and excel. Make sure to give regular updates throughout the month to keep them engaged. That will add the sizzle to make it as successful as possible.

In-store contests are also effective. A contest to sell the most monthly specials might be the perfect opportunity to raise sales and achieve the store goal this month. Prizes don't have to be expensive to be effective. A paid weekend off or a $50 gift card might do very nicely. Free company shirts are usually a hit as well.

Contests work. They're good for morale and your business. Utilize them to get that extra boost every store needs from time to time.

A Foundation of Fundamentals

The solid foundation of your business is what keeps it strong. It's made up of the many fundamental practices you've trained your employees to perform without exception. Spotless restrooms, appealing displays and a friendly staff all play a role in offering your customers the same outstanding experience every time they shop in your store. Just like the tallest skyscrapers, your business will collapse without a strong foundation.

Just because Nick has worked in your bowling alley for over a year, that doesn't mean he still cleans and polishes the lanes every day like you trained him. Water will always travel the path of least resistance. In his mind, it may seem perfectly acceptable to take a few shortcuts and save a little time. The extra effort required to make sure these lanes stay perfect isn't really necessary anymore. He's found a better way.

Your job is to periodically check behind your employees to make sure they consistently execute the fundamentals. Don't be the type of manager who makes the mistake of thinking everyone surely knows this by now, and it doesn't require your attention. They will all need reminding from time to time.

It doesn't matter what changes your business goes through or how busy your store gets from 4 p.m. until 6 p.m. Your employees should understand you expect the fundamentals to be adhered to every day. If you stop checking behind them on a regular basis to make sure this happens, you'll wake up one day and realize your store doesn't serve as many customers as it once did. Your foundation of fundamentals has eroded away, and some customers stopped giving you their business. If that happens, it's probably a good time to retrain your employees on the basics that made you successful.

Payroll and Scheduling

Cost control is part of everyday life for a store manager. Monitoring portions, waste and shrinkage all contribute to making a healthy net profit. Payroll, however, is usually the largest **controllable cost**. Every minute of every working day is about keeping those dollars in line with the budget.

The manager is usually given a payroll limit based on a percentage of projected sales. As an example, if your store is projected to make $20,000 in sales for the week and you have been assigned a 10% payroll limit, then you'll have $2000 to operate the store and properly serve all your customers. Make your schedule using a lesser dollar figure to expect the unexpected. The challenges are to incorporate sick time, vacations or lack of staff into the work week. Make the payroll total $50 or $100 less than budget to give yourself a little cushion.

Use all the tools at your disposal. Sales per day or per hour are necessary figures to properly allocate staffing levels. If Fridays generate 25% of total weekly sales, then 25% of payroll dollars should be spent on Fridays.

Your weekly planner comes into play here, as well. Who's receiving training? What special tasks need to be completed? Anything out of the ordinary should be addressed.

The next step is to make a rough draft of the schedule. Use a pencil. Unless you're a rare breed of manager, you'll make mistakes and changes before you're finished. Erasers are a blessing.

Don't schedule full-time employees for 40 hours. You don't want them to report to work at exactly 9 a.m. as scheduled. They'll normally show up a little early to get situated before they clock in. If they clock in early or work late, every extra minute is overtime. Nothing will torpedo a payroll budget more quickly than overtime. Then someone will have some explaining to do. Always schedule full-time employees for 38 or 39 hours per week as a safeguard.

Check the employee hours worked once or twice a week. If business is more or less than anticipated, adjust accordingly. If someone has worked extra time, you can reduce his or her hours over the rest of the week to stay within the budget.

The work schedule may need to change over time for various reasons. Four new employees are starting this week to open the store and the schedule needs to allow time for learning and developing. After a month of training, you realize only two employees are needed. You might bring the other two employees back a little later when business picks up. If you're the manager of a greeting card store and you know Valentine's Day is coming up, you'll expect the days leading up to it to be very busy. Whatever the case, review the schedule weekly and adjust as needed.

Reviewing the schedule is also the time to explore the possibility of hiring part-time employees. The work schedule is so much easier to make with the greater flexibility part-time employees allow. Vacations and sick time aren't as much of a burden. Another lawn and garden specialist during spring months or an extra set of hands on stock day helps overall efficiency and customer service. A fireman who works four days a week could very well be one of your best employees on the other three days he's available. He's just trying to earn a little extra income and could work as little or as often as needed.

Change is Coming

Last year's fashion is definitely not in for this year. The new menu has an expanded selection of lunch specials. Based on modern technology, these new golf clubs are lighter and stronger than a few years ago, so they've been added to the inventory. Ashton just got promoted to another store and Rebekah just quit her waitressing job so she could go to college. Next week is computer training for everyone on the new system. In the world of business, change is always coming.

Businesses have to change. Old products and outdated services won't go very far in serving the customer of today. Customers evolve and always expect more, so businesses have to try new and updated products and services to not only keep up with their competitors, but to attempt to gain an advantage over them. Sometimes the changes work and sometimes they don't. Either way, it's time to learn and move on. Rather than being afraid of change, be afraid of working for a business that always stays the same. Have you ever watched a 20-year-old television show and noticed how dated the clothes and cars would be today? Do you want to be the manager of any store that still sells them? Not only would customers not shop with you, they would laugh as they walked by your store.

Everyone gains a certain comfort level with their surroundings and their routines. Whether you realize it or not, over the years you've become stable and secure in your personal life. The place you shop for groceries, those old blue jeans in the back of the closet and your circle of friends are the same. But wanting to keep things the same can work against you when you're the manager, because you're an instrument of necessary changes. If you question every change, or even worse, relay those feelings to your employees, you'll have an entire staff who's resistant to change. The end result will be a lack of necessary progress for your store.

Be positive about change and do your best to understand it. Relay that positive attitude to your employees. Upper-level managers usually don't ask for change unless they've pondered the matter exhaustively and deemed it best for your business. Get excited. New times are ahead of you. Lead your employees to facilitate whatever change your company requires to keep pace with the marketplace. If you don't, you'll be the only manager of the last-standing cassette tape store in North America.

Think Outside the Box

Albert Einstein once said, "The definition of insanity is doing the same thing over and over and expecting different results." Any manager can have difficulty seeing the business as a whole while mired in the day-to-day tasks of operating it. The end result is a routine of doing the same things over and over. Make the new schedule by noon. Order the sale merchandise by the 3 p.m. cut-off time. Change the oil in the fryers every Thursday. Therein lies the life of the average manager until something changes.

Every now and again, take a step back from all of that and look at your store from a different point of view. Is there a better way to accomplish something? Can you be more efficient or give better service? Imagine you're a customer or a competitor and look at your store through that person's eyes. It's called thinking outside the box.

Periodically visit your competitors. Analyze them inside and out. Do they offer products or services your company could be offering at a superior quality or better price? What do they do better or worse than you? Can you learn something from them today to try in your store?

There are new ideas and better practices to be learned from most any business, if you pay attention. A car wash can learn from a convenience store and vice versa. Take notice when you go into any business. Something can be learned there.

If you try ten new things, and five of them work and five don't, did you do a good thing or a bad thing? You did a great thing! You implemented five new ideas to improve your business. It doesn't get much better than that.

Innovation can also come from within. Have some reward system for employees who submit new ideas to improve the business in some way. You might be surprised as to how good some of those ideas really are. Remember, they want to contribute to the team effort, as well, to share in your store's success.

When the time comes to seek better results, look at things from a different point of view. The answers could be all around you.

Dealing with Stress

You planned your week to perfection and everything is on schedule. Sales are up 17%, the cashier outages have drastically improved and your store is in first place in the contest. On a personal note, you finally got your grass cut yesterday and your daughter got a much-needed 100 on her math test. Life is good. You came to work ready to conquer the world. Then it happens. Kaboom! The ship hits an iceberg.

The air conditioning system just stopped working and the high today is 96! Your supervisor called and asked for a complete inventory of discontinued merchandise by the end of the day. One of the delivery drivers called in sick and your assistant manager just informed you that you're out of register tape. Everybody should head for the hills! This store needs a manager.

Step one is to remain calm. If you can maintain your composure while everyone else is losing theirs, then you're truly in charge. Think through the tasks that need to be done and get the help you need. It's all around you. Ask your assistant manager to call the air conditioning repair company to see what time a service tech can arrive to repair the problem. Ask the other two delivery drivers for their help.

The business needs them to perform at a higher level today and get ready for the store's busy times. Instruct the cashier to call the office supply store to purchase register tape.

The manager can only do so much planning. Circumstances will arise that require a composed manager who's thinking clearly to address each situation head on. Acting like you've lost your mind or demonstrating absolutely no ability to rectify what's happened won't help anyone. Becoming emotional and letting these situations get the best of you will only cloud your good judgment. Your employees will see these shortcomings and know you're not the type of leader to handle these setbacks. It doesn't matter why the ship hit an iceberg. The fact is, it did. So stay calm, think through the problems and handle them one by one by using everyone necessary to help you solve them.

Ask For Help

Too often, managers get promoted and don't want to appear weak or give the impression they don't know what they should. Here's a hint: The person who promoted you already knows this. You've got to be the one to figure that out. You weren't promoted because you knew it all. You were promoted because you demonstrated the ability to follow the company's direction, excelled in personal performance and did what was necessary to make yourself the clear choice for advancement.

The "problem managers" want to operate in a bubble to figure out everything on their own. This is where the real problems occur. How foolish is that? Use the knowledge at your disposal. That's how you learn and develop.

There's no greater sense of relief for your supervisor than to know you'll call and ask for advice if you have a problem. Teaching you becomes so much easier and a lot of mistakes are avoided if you aren't afraid to ask questions.

There will also be times when you need help but don't know it. Communication is the key here. Keep your supervisor apprised as much as you can. Discuss your goals and plans. Talk about the business in general and employee development. Your supervisor once wore the manager tag and lived through your experience, so soak up that knowledge. Try to combine everything you know with everything your supervisor knows. You'll progress so much faster as a store manager if you simply ask for help every time you even think you need it.

Achieving Balance

Do your absolute best to achieve that happy balance in life. Your role as a manager shouldn't be everything to you. Working 80 hours per week will not only lessen your effectiveness, it will completely burn you out. You'll get tired of the job or lose your focus, and either quit or get fired.

Many times your position will require extra time and effort because you're responsible for getting the job done. The manager's schedule is only a starting point during some weeks. Training a new staff or remodeling your store is both time-consuming and necessary.

This is exactly the reason any store manager needs to take the proper time off. Recharge your batteries. Do the rest of the things in life that matter to you. Play hopscotch with your children. Take your wife on a date. Make plans with an old friend you haven't seen in months. When you get back to work, you'll be refreshed. The tension that sometimes builds will lessen. The world is a better place, and you're ready to lead like you're capable.

Don't be short-sighted and your own worst enemy. You didn't accept the job as manager for the short term. Long-term success and achievement should be the goal, but that won't happen if you become the bright star that burns out in a short period of time. The store manager needs time off for rest and relaxation just like everybody else. Use it to fulfill the other areas in your life that are important, as well.

*

Use your own personal touch when
you see fit to express your gratitude for
hard work or achievement.

*

Part 2

Your Employees

Your Employees

You were the best employee. You knew the job better than anyone else in the company. Your accomplishments were duly noted, and you got promoted to store manager. Congratulations! Now what? Being promoted to store manager doesn't make you a manager. Now you'll need your employees' help to keep this job.

How does a human being transform him- or herself from a person who is used to being a successful employee, to a person who takes the ultimate pride in watching someone he or she trained to achieve that same level of success? The answer is understanding the fact that employees outnumber you and **your store operates through them**. You're the force behind the scenes. It's about you, but it's not about you. Your knowledge and skills mean nothing if you can't pass them on to your employees. When they succeed, you succeed. Their goals and dreams should become your priority. You're the manager, coach and trainer. How you handle those roles will determine your level of success.

Make it your personal business to understand why each employee works in your store. They really do want to tell you, and you can learn every last detail by listening carefully.

You'll then understand everything you need to know to manage a successful business through them. Have you ever heard of W.I.I.F.M? It stands for "What's in it for me?" It means your employees always want to know how they benefit from your management direction and decisions. Your job is to help them find that very answer.

Demonstrate a genuine interest in the well-being and overall development of each and every employee. Create a work environment that promotes a team atmosphere where everyone feels important. Use the word "we" whenever you talk about topics concerning the business. By providing encouragement, training and setting the proper example, your reward will be to manage a group of productive employees who are content in their work, and with you.

Assistant Managers

The definition of quid pro quo literally means "something for something" (you help me and I help you). This is supposed to be the working relationship between a manager and his or her assistant managers. The manager's responsibility is to train the assistant manager to one day become a manager. The assistant's responsibility is to perform some of the management functions, and make a diligent attempt to listen, learn and put into practice all of the necessary skills to correctly manage a store.

The assistant manager doesn't, however, act as a servant. Performing every task the manager doesn't want to do, or working every lousy shift on the schedule without any real training doesn't benefit anyone. If it happened to you, don't pass it on. The goal of a good manager should be to teach the assistant all of the attributes necessary to be promoted to store manager.

Osmosis doesn't train an assistant manager. If simply watching everything you do was sufficient, then anyone who watched baseball enough times on the television and hung around the local ball park could play center field for the New York Yankees.

Of course it doesn't work that way. So what does? Your relentless efforts to teach your assistants how to become a store manager, is the only answer.

Planning your week, making a proper schedule and implementing efficient systems should all be in place so you can actually spend time teaching your assistants how to perform well and progress like you did. Train your assistants how to make a schedule or let them run the staff meeting as you look on. If it doesn't go well, point out the positives and correct the areas that require attention afterward. They need to understand your weekly planner, be involved with the goals and learn to train employees.

You'll then have assistant managers who are truly part of the management staff and can offer solid assistance and participation in running a profitable business. What greater feeling of satisfaction could there be than one day realizing four other managers with your company used to be your assistant managers? You trained them well and knew they were ready to lead fellow employees and manage a store of their own. When the time came, you gave your personal recommendation for promotion. The day that happens, someone probably has his or her eye on you for promotion, as well.

Your Stories

How about those stories some managers love to tell? They can speak for hours on the grand tales of their rise to fame and glory back in the day. As a staff member, they were the best, the fastest and they never made mistakes. A picture of certain managers receiving the golden knife award for being the fastest oyster shucker in Omaha for 2006 adorns the office wall. There are managers who can add some great personal past achievement to any conversation, and they want employees to be more like they were.

Here's a news flash: Never do that because your employees don't care about your stories. They want to benefit and learn from your expertise, but not at the expense of enduring you showing off pictures of your trophy case. You'll generate an equal amount of enthusiasm by describing your personal technique for parking your car perfectly straight between the lines. None.

Your employees already know you're the manager, not the best tire changer in the company anymore. They realize you had success in the past. Your job now is to utilize your knowledge and experience to train them to become successful like you were, but leave the stories of your past greatness at home.

Cell Phones

The invention of the cell phone has truly changed the world forever. It has enabled everyone to communicate, wherever they might be, and retrieve enormous amounts of information with the touch of a button. We have the ability to text, talk, tweet and tune in 24 hours a day. It happens at the mall, the ball game, driving a 4,000-pound SUV and, yes, at work. Everyone is dying to know if Wanda had her baby. Let's check Facebook. Mark's favorite football team plays at 4 and it's a must-see game.

The downside comes when employees bring their cell phones to work and talk on them all day. Every minute employees are on their cell phone at the same time they're on the time clock is a wasted minute. When these minutes are added up, in light of the unlimited calling plans available, that's a lot of wasted minutes.

Make sure you write a store policy stating all personal cell phones must be turned off while at work, and place this notice in the employee handbook. If Norma complains that no one can contact her in the event of an emergency, gently explain how a land line works.

Norma has a job. She can tell her family and friends where she works, and if the message is important, they can call the business landline. Since she can't stay on the business phone all day because it has no apps to play with, she has to work her shift with no interruptions and text her friends when she gets off. That's a great beginning to a productive day for Norma and the business.

Clear Expectations

It seems obvious. Be clear about how you expect your employees to perform their jobs. Explain the who, what, where, when, why and how of everything they need to know to serve your customers at a high level. So what's the problem? Why do surveys reveal a lot of employees are dissatisfied with their supervisor because they don't understand what's expected of them? How can any store manager not perform this fundamental duty properly?

It happens because it's not as simple as it seems. You have a lot to cover with your employees, and disseminating that much information can be a tall task. There are company policies, store goals, training, and the list goes on. Informing and teaching the people who work for you is a part of the job that never ends. If your message isn't clear or your employees don't fully comprehend what you said, they won't understand what you expect. Either way, they'll become disgruntled with you, and rightfully so.

There's something that must be a part of every staff meeting, one-on-one meeting and on-the-job-training. That something is **feedback**. It's the only way you can truly know what they learned.

Soliciting useful feedback isn't asking things like "Any questions?" or "You got it?" A head nod isn't going to tell you anything. Instead, try saying "Repeat back to me what I just said." That may seem silly, but you'll quickly learn it's the best way. There will be times when you find yourself repeating something two or three times before the person truly understands it enough to repeat it back to you.

Take the time to thoroughly explain every topic you need to cover. Get feedback and answer questions to make sure your message is clear and understood. You need a discussion, not a lecture. By doing this, your employees will always know exactly what you expect and can perform their jobs accordingly. Sounds like a good place to work!

Listen

Listening is a funny thing. You do it every day, or at least you think you do. Your friends, the baby crying and all those people you hear at work and home require your attention. So do you listen, or do you hear with a smile and pretend you're listening?

Many years ago, a global manufacturer performed a study and asked all the employees in one of the company plants, "What can we do to make your job better?" The goal was to measure the results of promoting employee participation in matters affecting the business.

The majority of the employees stated the lighting was too dim to work effectively. So the company decided to act on the suggestion and installed brighter lights over the assembly line. What do you think happened? Productivity went up 10%. The results seemed obvious. The company asked its employees what it could do to make their jobs better, received their feedback, gave them what they wanted and their productivity increased.

The company then decided to continue the study and, several months later, reduced the lighting levels to their original state. What do you think happened then? **Productivity continued to go up!** It sounds backward, or does it?

There are more than 7 billion people in the world, and each of them wants to feel important. The employees' concern was about the lighting, but at the same time, it wasn't about the lighting. They wanted to feel like they were part of a company that recognized the fact that each and every employee's opinion should matter and be heard. Because that actually happened, they felt a greater sense of satisfaction and participation with their job, and increased productivity was the result.

It's not that you're the manager and now have to act upon the employee's input every time one of them offers it. But you do have to listen. Put down your pen and hang up your phone when they speak to you. Give every employee your undivided attention when he or she is asking a question or making a point. Maybe you'll act, or maybe you won't, but the point is you gave their input respect by demonstrating with your actions and words that you really do care what they think.

Your employees make up the stones and mortar of your business. They wait on the customers and do their jobs every day. This allows them the opportunity to see things from the employee's point of view. They might actually discover a better or faster way to accomplish something you hadn't considered. There will be times when their input will actually help your store, if you would simply take the time to really listen to what they have to say. Their input is very valuable to your store, so listen and act like it.

Praise in Public – Correct in Private

This is a guideline you should never break. Praise your employees in public as often as you can, and always take corrective action in private. The first part is easy to understand. Who wants to ride on a parade float with nobody watching or model the latest fashions down a runway to empty chairs? Is there a difference between hitting a home run in batting practice with a few hundred people watching and hitting a home run in the bottom of the ninth inning with 40,000 fans screaming? You'd better believe there is. So how do you use those basic human emotions and desires to better serve your store?

Complimenting your employees in front of co-workers or customers will multiply their effect tenfold. Some people will walk three feet off the ground for a week after getting recognized for good work in front of others. They'll work late, perform extra duties or go the extra mile to do whatever it takes to keep those types of praises coming.

Imagine you're the manager of a high volume coffee shop and during the height of the morning rush, you notice everyone working very hard and all the orders are hot, fast and perfect.

What if you say something like "Thanks everyone." "You're doing a great job." in front of all the customers. Most of your employees will then work even faster and harder than before. The positive effects of a public praise like that on productivity, morale and team spirit are almost immeasurable. Try it and see.

It'll be the guillotine for you if you break this one: Always correct your employees in private, without exception. Discuss the problem one-on-one with no one else listening. You can do no greater harm to employee morale or create ill will for a particular individual than to lose your head and correct him or her in public. It's disrespectful and will never reap any rewards. In fact, some employees may start performing even worse just to get you back. If you make this mistake, your only hope of redemption is to let the dust settle, all the heads clear and apologize to your employee in front of everyone the same way you scolded him or her earlier. Hopefully, that will fix your error so you can move forward and never make the same mistake again.

Show Appreciation

If you believe that because you're the store manager, every time you ask an employee to perform a task it will be done properly, you will quickly learn this is not the case. They have to want to do it and believe you will notice and appreciate them when they do it well.

Words like "please" and "thank you" demonstrate basic respect and are a great starting point, but they're not enough. Compliment achievements and hard work. Make sure your employees understand you couldn't do this job without them. **Show them your appreciation.**

There are also other ways to say thank you. Order pizza or subs once a month at lunch time. Bring coffee and doughnuts to an early morning staff meeting. Insert handwritten notes into the paycheck envelopes thanking your employees for all the hard work. Keep a list of birthdays in your weekly planner and wish them a happy birthday.

Use your own personal touch when you see fit to express your gratitude. A small gesture can go a long way in building a team of satisfied and productive employees. Never miss an opportunity to show your genuine appreciation with your words and your actions.

Motivation

What makes one football coach get more out of the same players than the previous coach did a year ago? Hollywood makes a lot of movies about a hardship that befalls a team or a player where the remaining players rally to support the cause. As a result, new heights never before achieved are now realized. "Win one for the Gipper."

It would appear that once motivated, most everyone has the ability to focus and try harder. The goal has been realized and nothing will get in the way. So what brings out that magic feeling that makes people really want to perform? What makes a person who knows how to do the job actually want to do the job? Is it simple or is it complicated?

You can read one of many books, each of which will show you a different way. There's also a lot of information online. Blank surveys are available to hand out so management can simply tally up the responses and understand what motivates employees. There are motivational speakers to inspire us to work harder, lose weight, set goals and a thousand other things. So where do you start and what do you do?

A lot of people think money is the ultimate motivator. Money is the be-all and end-all to motivation. If you think that way, then take this deal and figure out how it ends. You're given everything money can buy to live out the rest of your life on one condition: you're now the only person on Earth. Suddenly there's no one to show that new Ferrari to. What's the point of having the 38-acre estate with four in-ground pools? The exotic beach just somehow lost its luster. Talking to a volleyball as if it were your best friend is no fun. Humans need to interact with other people to acquire their own personal sense of belonging. Money is obviously important because it keeps the lights on, but it's not the only thing that motivates people.

Fear and intimidation can motivate someone for sure, but they don't produce sustained motivation. People will usually run faster while being chased by a lion, and sell more add-on items after the threat of being fired, but after a while they're right back where they started.

Every employee is unique. Take the time to listen and learn what each one considers important, so you'll then understand what it takes to truly motivate your staff. Most of the time they won't have to say a word. You'll already know.

People want to:
- Matter
- Contribute
- Be heard
- Be challenged
- Be rewarded
- Get noticed
- Be part of a team
- Help others
- Feel important
- Have the money to live and provide

George always volunteers to help because he wants to contribute and be part of the team. Let him know you appreciate his team spirit. Rhonda seems to walk three feet off of the ground with a great big smile every time you tell her what a great job she's doing. Keep those compliments going her way. Rick needs some discipline from time to time to keep his sales where they need to be. He usually knows it's coming, and wants to be challenged to perform at a higher level. Let him know you appreciate his efforts, but his productivity must remain consistent.

Motivating your employees isn't a "one size fits all." What's important to one person may mean absolutely nothing to the next. Try to recognize the difference between an employee who constantly offers suggestions to improve your store because you listen, and another who'll walk through a blizzard to get to work because you always compliment how great he or she is with customers. When you can do that, your employees will be motivated to work harder for you than they ever have before. Guaranteed.

Look For Changes

This topic is a little more subtle than some of the others, but it's still important. It deals with you noticing changes in employee behavior or performance. Those changes usually signal a problem of which you should be aware. When they begin to affect the business negatively, it's time for you to become involved in an attempt to solve them. Some examples might be:

- John has never been late in the last six months. Now he comes in late almost every other day.
- Tammy's money count at the end of her shift has always been within a dollar but lately she's lucky to be only ten dollars off.
- Jenny has been the top salesperson for more than a year, but this summer she struggles just to make the top ten.

Have a private discussion with the employee and express your concerns. Point out the changes you've noticed and try to find out what's causing them. Get all the facts and offer your guidance, so that together you can work to resolve the problem.

You may find that John saw no future with your store and has been interviewing with other companies for two weeks. You now have the opportunity to discuss his performance and future with the company. Tammy's just made some new friends and is staying out until 4 a.m. on most nights. Her concentration level isn't what it once was. You'll want to point out the importance of her job and recommend she only stay out late before her days off. Jenny's mother just became very ill and she's spending most of her free time caring for her. You might suggest a leave of absence until things return to normal.

You're not trying to pry into your employees' personal affairs. You're trying to run a profitable business. That means everyone needs to be free from distractions that would prevent them from performing at a high level. Life also happens off the time clock, and occasionally it will require your expertise to help an employee and your store.

The Art of Training

Make no mistake. Training is an art. It takes time to learn and master. You'll constantly learn new ways to do it better and more efficiently if you try. The ability to teach people is a powerful trait to possess.

The dictionary defines *training* as follows:

1. To make proficient by instruction and practice.
2. To develop or form the habits, thoughts or behavior by discipline and instruction.

So how do you actually train someone? How do you teach an employee to know what you know and put that knowledge to good use in performing his or her job?

Further complicating matters is the fact that everyone learns at different speeds. The average person has to hear something between three and seven times to remember it. So does Paul have to hear it three or seven times? If you train him on five things, which three did he remember and which two did he forget?

Telling and *training* are two different words because they mean two different things.

How many times have you clearly told an employee how to do something and the very next day he or she did it incorrectly? What was your first thought? Could this person simply be slow or not care? Perhaps the answer lies in a different direction. You were a poor trainer. Let's fix that right now and for good.

Before we review the proven steps to make you a better trainer, we'll cover some helpful guidelines to remember before you begin.

1. Plan for training: Make a daily training agenda, including any ideas or special thoughts you wish to cover. Have everything you need, like props or reference sheets, to illustrate your point properly.
2. Set aside time for training: You can't effectively train anyone in between customers or phone calls. Have the fewest interruptions possible so the training session will be meaningful.
3. Don't give more information than your employees can absorb at one time. Every hour you add to a training session means the trainee retention rate goes down. There's nothing you can ever do to change that. Be informative and brief.

4. Ask the trainees to take notes or provide handouts pertaining to the topics you'll be covering that day. This will give them a reference to study later.
5. Never let an employee perform the training unless you've personally taught this person to train and train well. It's a recipe for disaster. It may seem logical or save time, but in the end your employees won't understand the training that's been covered, and you'll have no idea who really understands what.

Let's review the steps that will make you an extraordinary trainer when you follow them:

- Step 1: Tell them
- Step 2: Show them
- Step 3: Let them do it
- Step 4: Commend what they did right and correct what they did wrong.
- Step 5: Repeat the process until they learn it.
- Step 6: Follow up for the next several days to make sure they retained the information.

The most common mistake is to combine steps one and two. You should avoid that whenever possible, because our brains can't think about two things at exactly the same time. Try to think about how bright the sun is and how dark the moon is at exactly the same time. You can't do it.

The same thing happens when you tell and show at the same time. The trainee will certainly retain some of both, but will comprehend so much more if you keep the two separated as much as possible. Have you ever watched a movie for a second or third time and realized you missed something the last time you saw it? That's a perfect example of what happens when a person has to watch and listen at the same time. First you explain the topic, then you show them how to do it.

The first five steps of training will be far less effective if you don't follow up every time to check what your employees remembered. Without it, you'll have no idea who actually retained the material you covered. Begin every new day of training with follow-up. Ask questions about previously covered material. Anything that's not completely understood should be reviewed again. If the whole training day becomes nothing but review, so be it. You need to monitor everyone's progress and adjust the training schedule accordingly.

By following the steps of training, you'll create a knowledgeable staff and your store will run like a well-oiled machine. The customers will enjoy doing business with you and your reward will be managing a thriving store with a healthy net profit.

Cross-training

This subject will most certainly help lessen the stress of being a manager. Cross-train as many employees as possible. Teach everyone in your store to perform multiple job functions.

If the cashiers are the only employees who know how to run the register other than yourself, and the auto parts salespeople are the only ones who can look up the correct parts, you're setting yourself up for the great fall. The stress and chaos will show up when the cashier calls in sick, and no one else can be reached. (It should be noted in the employee handbook that everyone should first try to find his or her replacement before calling in sick- hint). When that happens, if you're the only one left who knows how to run the register, then it looks like you won't be doing much managing that day.

By cross-training everyone, when a salesperson goes on vacation, you'll have trained substitutes in all your cashiers. When you decide to promote an employee to assistant manager because your current assistant got promoted to manage another store across town, you'll have a pool of possible candidates who already work there.

Look how many things fall right into place when employees learn multiple job descriptions.

Teach the truck loader the delivery route. Show the deli manager how to display produce. Look at every area of your store and make sure several people know how to perform every job. That way sick days, vacations or promotions won't disrupt the smooth flow of your store. You then get to be the manager and not a temporary fill-in.

Delegating With Follow-up

Most store managers are working managers. They have to perform some of the daily store functions to keep the payroll budget in line with the goals. They might have to serve customers, fill in at the cash register during lunch or lend a hand to unload the stock truck. Whatever it takes, they are there to help.

They also have management duties to perform like schedules, security and training. Needless to say, there's a lot to accomplish every day, and every manager needs help from the employees to make sure the business runs smoothly.

It's foolish and counterproductive to overload yourself with duties and responsibilities that other employees could handle. If you perform certain tasks because you believe you're the only person who can do them properly, then you're a poor trainer. If "things to do" seem to pile up in your lap all the time, then your weekly planning skills might need some work.

Tasks that can be delegated should be. Make a duties list and assign them to your staff. Some examples might be washing the windows, checking the a/c filters or changing the message on the road sign. Post it in a conspicuous place. Periodically change the person responsible for each task so your employees know how to perform many of them. The unexpected will always occur, and additional tasks might need to be delegated throughout the week, as well.

Some of your management duties should also be delegated when the time is right. Once your assistant managers have demonstrated the ability to assume additional responsibilities, **let them**. Hopefully, your previous manager taught you how to place the stock order and make the work schedule. He or she took a chance and delegated a new responsibility to you, and then cared enough to check behind you to make sure you learned to do it well. It's time to pay it forward. Not only should you delegate tasks to your assistant managers and follow up every time, you should also teach them how to delegate with follow-up to store employees. They'll never become a successful store manager without understanding its importance.

Which glamorous city will you visit on your vacation if you're the only person in the store who performs all the management functions? You shouldn't travel very far, because you'll probably have to come back early to handle something.

Once the delegation process is complete, you're only halfway there. Now you must follow up as many times as it takes to make sure every employee clearly understood how to perform the job and actually completed it at an acceptable level. You're wasting valuable time if you ask anyone to do anything and don't follow up every time. It doesn't matter how busy your schedule is. **Don't delegate it unless you can follow up on your request!**

No job is too small for the proper follow-up. Ask yourself if a certain task can be done improperly. If the answer is yes, then it requires your follow-up. Can the dumpster fill up too early in the week if the boxes aren't broken down? Follow up to make sure employees always break down the boxes first. Will the floors be clean if an employee doesn't use enough soap in the mop water? Follow up again to make sure every last detail is done properly.

You might be amazed at how many basic duties no one ever really taught your employees. By following up on everything you ask, you'll be able to teach them the proper way to perform their jobs from the ground up. You'll then have a group of people who are part of the team because they're each in charge of various duties, and you care enough to check and make sure they perform their jobs well.

Some employees will notice what you do and actually thank you for taking the time to teach them the right way to perform their duties. The first day that happens, a little light bulb should go on. You'll begin to realize this way of managing is both different and better. It feels good to help people by putting them in charge of something, noticing how they did it and teaching them to do it well. You're now starting to understand what it takes to become a successful manager.

Relaying Information

You open the mail from corporate headquarters or your supervisor calls to tell you about an upcoming change. Starting this Friday, your company will no longer sell brand X shirts, and your store must send the remaining inventory back by Monday. The next staff meeting isn't until Tuesday, so it can't wait until then. Your store has 23 employees working on two different shifts. How do you inform everyone of that one piece of information?

If the only method of communication in your store is to tell everyone about the change, then that's a colossal waste of time. What sense does it make to say the same thing 23 times? Even if it's only 15 times, it's still a waste. There must be a better way to utilize those 480 minutes today.

Getting the message out via bulletin board is not effective enough. Some notices hang there until they fade or fall off, so employees don't pay attention to it daily. Even if most employees look at it most of the time, does that guarantee 23 people will know about brand X by Friday?

You need a better system. (There's that word again). Somewhere near the time clock, set up trays or slots for each employee. Train everyone to check his or her slot before clocking in. That way you can make a copy of the notice and put it in everyone's slot. Now you've made the announcement in far less time than passing along the same message 23 times, and everyone knows about brand X. You might also use this type of communication to distribute new name tags, upcoming schedule changes, thank you notes or a hundred other things. It's a timesaver.

You can also send smaller messages via text or email. Set up two different contact groups. The first group should be managers only. That way you can send messages specific to them. The second group should include all employees so you can send messages on issues affecting everyone. Ask for a response so you know they've read it. Your total time invested would be about 30 seconds. That's efficient and effective communication to relay all types of information in the least amount of time.

Staff Meetings

Staff meetings are necessary and time well spent. By having the entire group together, your message reaches everyone at once. You need to set the store's direction and review your expectations of the day or week. Your goals should be to inform, train, and motivate.

Here are some guidelines about conducting a productive meeting:

- Be prepared with a list of topics you wish to cover. This will assist in getting out the most information in the least amount of time. Throughout the week, make a note each time you notice something that should be covered with the employees. Bill sells more high-end carpet than anyone else and you want him to explain how he does it. The new holiday schedule needs to be covered this week. Spring merchandise arrives on Thursday, and it's time to prepare to receive the inventory. What better time to address these topics than with everyone present?
- Set a time limit for the meeting and do your best to stick to it. Stay in charge and don't let the conversations stray too far off course.

- Get as much participation from the employees as possible. They will have ideas and suggestions which may benefit the group as well.
- It's always an excellent time to bring up employee successes and accomplishments. Lisa just received an award for being employee of the month and Jerry just received a promotion to assistant manager. How about a round of applause for those two!
- Never single out employees for poor performance or mistakes, and don't beat up the group. Stay positive. Your goal is to foster change, not make everyone feel incompetent.

Once you've gone over all the material, take a moment to sum up the meeting and thank your attendees for their time and participation. End on a positive note.

Try to understand just how very important staff meetings are. You can move mountains with these people if you try. Plan for them so your employees actually enjoy the time they spend learning and contributing. This is the time when you bond with them and they with you, so don't waste it. It's like the family dinner of your business, so make the most of it.

Interviewing & Hiring

An influx of competent and motivated new employees can really change the face and direction of the business. The store runs smoother, sales gets better and the customers are happier.

When the time comes to hire a new employee, you should first review the applications to form a list of potential candidates. Then schedule a time for the interviews when you'll not be disturbed. Never be late for the appointment. It makes a poor first impression of your company. Not only are you trying to figure out if this person would be a good fit for the store, but the candidate is also trying to figure out if he or she wants to work for your company.

Take the first several minutes to allow the prospect to relax and let down his or her guard a bit. You're in your element and comfortable, so allow a little adjustment time. Ask about the weather, current events or anything that gets the conversation off to a good start with dialogue going both ways. You can learn a lot about this person's likes, dislikes or general habits right from the start if you listen.

Next, gather some basic information like which position the candidate is applying for, method of transportation and scheduling preferences. You might be interviewing for a full-time cashier, and this candidate may only be able to work three days a week. Don't rule anyone out immediately. If they're qualified, then maybe two part-time cashiers will give you greater flexibility than one full-time.

Ask questions you might have about the application and fill in any missing details. This leads to covering broader topics like previous employment, future aspirations and personal talents this person could bring to the job.

Salary is almost always an important topic, so check to see whether the salary offered for this job is in line with the prospect's past salaries. You don't want to hire someone who might be using this position as a stepping-stone until a better offer comes along.

The more information you gather, the better the decision you'll make. Try to ask open-ended questions which don't require a yes or no answer. You want your interviewee to expound upon any answer he or she chooses. Some examples might be:

- "Tell me about yourself."
- "What did you like or dislike about your last job?"
- "What will your previous employer say about your job performance?"

After you've gathered all the information you need to make your hiring decision, ask for any questions about your company or the available position. Then let the candidate know how and when you'll inform everyone about your decision, and follow through with it. Be polite and thank the person for his or her time. Everyone you decide not to hire should still be treated respectfully. They might actually end up being your customers.

If you're still interested after the interview, call previous employers and references to gather additional information about past performance and personality traits. Drug screenings and background checks are a good idea.

Never take shortcuts in the interviewing and screening process. Some people can be very deceptive, and your instincts about how the candidate will perform could be dead wrong. If all goes well, however, you've put yourself in the best possible position to hire the most qualified and productive person for the job.

The worst thing you can do is hire someone out of desperation. Having an inadequate staff doesn't mean you should offer a job to the first warm body who shows up. It's not fair to the company or the individual. Hiring the wrong person will create more problems than it solves. If you interview seven people in a row who aren't qualified for the job, then move on to number eight.

The solid foundation of your store can only be built with quality employees. The person you decide to hire will potentially serve thousands of your customers. So conduct thorough interviews for as long as it takes to find the best person for the job. You'll be glad you did.

Performance Evaluations

Most established companies have some type of standard performance review form. If your business doesn't have one, download or purchase one. Other than your daily training and mentoring, this is the most concrete way of giving the employees feedback on how you and the company view their performance. It puts something in their hands that measures achievements and areas that need improvement.

Plan for the reviews by keeping track of the dates they're due in your planner. If the review is late, there's usually very little you can do to make it right. A 90-day review means you give the review in 90 days, and an annual review means you give it on the employee's anniversary date, not two weeks later. Your apology may help, but you've already demonstrated you don't care enough or don't notice the work that employee does. Employees usually know the dates of their reviews.

Read the employee's file to remind yourself of the entire period being reviewed. Promotions, raises and the employee's continued development all depend on how you handle the evaluation.

Study each area of the review carefully and really give it some thought. If a particular area needs improvement, note it. If the performance in another area was stellar, state that, as well. The main goal is to be as truthful as you can and help your employees improve and develop.

Be sure to thank them for their efforts and congratulate their achievements. Clearly explain your expectations for the year ahead, and seize this moment to challenge them to achieve higher levels of success.

Above all, be fair. It's human nature to like one person more or less than another, but this is a business, so you must give an impartial evaluation. Treat each of your reviews with equal judgment. These individual evaluations of performance are important to your employees and should, therefore, make the process very important to you.

Pay for Performance

Most companies will allow the manager some latitude when it comes to awarding pay raises. He or she is on the front line of the business and usually knows the overachievers and the underachievers. Upper management will usually issue a guideline to control employee raises and maintain the store's payroll budget. You'll be the one to decide how much of a raise is given to each employee when the time is right.

The pay raise should coincide with the performance evaluation. That way, your review of the employee's strengths and weaknesses has set the stage to explain how much of a raise he or she has truly earned. This is valuable one-on-one time with your employees. Their performance review, along with a salary evaluation, is a big deal to them because it only happens once a year, so you should treat it accordingly. Always take the time to make sure they're done properly.

This is not the time to be cheap. There are probably 500 other ways to save company money than to hold back a fifty-cents-an-hour raise to a deserving employee. If he or she follows your direction and serves the customers well, then pay for it. A pay raise should also accompany a request for greater efforts and additional responsibilities. Your competition would gladly give your best employees fifty cents more an hour to serve their customers properly. If you want a steak, then you have to pay for a steak.

You'll need a lot of good people to manage a successful business. What's the difference in sales between a store with an outstanding staff and a store with a mediocre one? Is it double, triple or more? If you do the math, you'll realize it's always in your best interest in the long run to pay good wages for good work. The end result will be the employee, the manager, the customer and the business, will all win.

Discipline

Your ability to administer timely and appropriate discipline to your employees lays the foundation that spells out how your store will operate. It offers structure and helps to enforce company rules and regulations. It's a necessary component of any successful store and its manager. If your only goal is to be well-liked, you'll never become an effective manager, and the business will suffer as a result. Your job is to earn respect by setting an example, while expecting effort with results.

Make your expectations clear. Explain the standards, policies and levels of performance you require from your employees, and enforce them without exception. These are non-negotiable. Making any request without enforcement is hollow. What's the point? There's nothing wrong with holding employees accountable for their actions. Every time you allow an opportunity for any area of the business to go downhill, it most certainly will. In some instances, the policies and procedures set forth by your company are put into place to ensure the very safety of the employees.

Hopefully, your company has a dress code. If someone shows up improperly dressed for work, send him or her home to change clothes. Don't make an exception. The message you send must be clear: no one will deviate from this policy. Do you believe this employee will show up improperly dressed for work again? Probably not. Your discipline in this matter also sends the same message to the rest of the staff: "Don't circumvent the dress code, or you, too, will be sent home."

The kitchen always stays this clean. Everyone reports to work on time. The floor displays stay stocked, cleaned and fronted at all times. Company policies are all put into place because they're in the best interest of your store and the employees. They apply to everyone, including the manager.

This doesn't mean, however, letting this authority go to your head and managing like Attila the Hun. Giving the impression that employees need to straighten up because there's a new sheriff in town, or threatening to fire everyone on most days, isn't discipline. It's a person with a manager title and an ego problem to deal with.

People who lack structure or discipline in their personal lives will actually want and appreciate it when they come to work. They'll be grateful for the fact you never waiver when it comes to your expectations of employee performance and results. At the end of the day, everyone leaves knowing they worked hard and performed their jobs well. You insisted they follow the rules and that's what's best for everyone involved. There'll be a sense of satisfaction and accomplishment among them because they know they work for both the right person and the right company.

Corrective Action

Occasionally, you'll need to sit down an employee in private to correct some type of performance or behavior, after several attempts to correct the problem by training or coaching have failed. The first step is to write it down on a correction form of some type. Be clear about what's wrong and how you expect the employee to correct the problem in the future. It should also clearly state any further action that may become necessary if corrective steps aren't taken. Include the date of a future meeting to discuss the progress, and write it in your weekly planner.

Reviewing this type of notice with your employees isn't supposed to be a punishment. It shouldn't become a lecture or a scolding. You should be trying to have a conversation that helps you better understand why this problem persists. Listen carefully and help in any reasonable way you can. The goal of this meeting should be to get your employee to understand the seriousness of the matter, and to make a commitment to rectify the situation.

End the meeting on a positive note. Review this person's strengths and abilities. Make it clear you have total confidence in him or her, and the issue should now be resolved. Give the employee a copy of the notice and place the other copy in the employee file.

In the days following the meeting, take the time to notice any improvements and compliment accordingly. Don't forget the follow-up meeting agreed upon. Hopefully, at that time you'll relay you're pleased with the progress and looking forward to more of the same.

Conflict Resolution

It sounds like a really big phrase for the simple fact that two or more people are having trouble agreeing on something. If you're a manager long enough, this is going to happen. You'll have to intervene and find an agreeable solution to settle a dispute between co-workers.

First of all, you must realize you can't put a group of people together for any length of time and always have complete harmony. From the first grade, to band camp, to the Capitol Building, people will have their differences. Some negotiating with a dash of common sense and the company's perspective will become necessary to find a solution. You didn't invent this dilemma, but you'll have to attempt to resolve it.

This is another one of those private conversations between the manager and the affected employees. Listen to each point of view and let everyone speak with little or no interruptions. When everyone's finished, you should ask questions to help you understand the situation completely.

Most of the time, the fix will be simple. Once everyone speaks their mind in a calm fashion and you step in with both your and the company's perspective, a reasonable and acceptable solution can be reached. Try to resolve the issue by the time everyone leaves the room, and make sure there are no hard feelings. Pay attention to what goes on for a week or two to make sure there are no relapses.

Termination

Despite the high hopes you had when you hired this person and all the time and effort you spent in training, this employee simply would not or could not do the job. So now you have to act in the best interest of the business. This is not a pleasant part of being a store manager, but it sometimes becomes necessary.

By the time you figure out you need to dismiss an employee, there should be signed documentation in his or her file, stating specific infractions of policies and procedures, along with the consequences if the problems weren't corrected. This is tangible proof of a justified employee dismissal.

A few points:

- Have the termination documentation prepared.
- Be courteous, respectful, and brief.
- The meeting should always be private.
- Don't discuss it with the other employees.
- Set guidelines for this person revisiting as a customer. Some kind of waiting period is usually a good idea.

Turnover

Talk about expensive! You need to hire a salesperson so you either run a newspaper ad or gather possible candidates from the website. Then you make phone calls to set up the interviews. After the interviews, you feel good about one person, so you offer the job and he accepts. On the day the new hire starts, all the paperwork needs to be completed and the employee manual must be covered in detail. Next, you need to introduce him properly to the staff and give a general tour of the store. He's put on the schedule, uniforms are issued and the list goes on. You finally filled the position and he's ready to start!

Over the next few weeks, you explain everything from the restrooms to the retail strategy. He shows up to work and seems to be catching on pretty well. The other employees like him and he's fitting in nicely. All the while this whole process is taking a lot of time and costing a lot of money.

Then after six weeks, for no apparent reason, the new hire quits. Someone is playing a bad joke! After all this time and money, the perfect prospect just up and quit? So now you have to perform the whole process over again.

What happens if you have to go through this entire process over and over again? People just seem to quit or get fired all the time. The actual costs can suffocate a business, to say nothing of the pure aggravation any manager experiences, and the perception by current employees that this might not be the best place to work.

If this problem persists in your store, it's not the quality of the candidates, contaminated water or some deep unsolved mystery in your city. Go straight to the top and stay there, because it's the manager, for sure. Something's wrong and it needs to be addressed immediately. Your eyes and ears may both deceive you, but the results remain obvious. People can't or won't work there.

Did you skip calling the references because you felt so good about this candidate? How about the fact he had worked three jobs over the past year? Were you too busy to conduct the training yourself, so you trusted an employee to do it?

The fundamentals explained in this book are vital to managing a successful store. Conducting thorough interviews, checking references, manager-led training, delegating with follow-up and so on, are all necessary to attract and keep quality employees. Excessive turnover is one of the ultimate results of not practicing them. Be the store manager who always adheres to the fundamentals on a daily basis, because employees are a whole lot cheaper to keep than to replace.

Summary

Being promoted to store manager is truly an accomplishment. You now join a league of talented men and women who've been chosen to lead and develop fellow employees to operate a profitable business. That doesn't happen every day or to everyone. No one ever promised this level of responsibility was going to be quick and easy. It requires time, effort and study, coupled with successes and failures. Your passion for this job, and the principles that guide you, have made all of this possible.

By purchasing this book, you've made a commitment to learn and develop. That's an awesome first step. Read it as many times as necessary to remind yourself of the fundamental techniques and people skills necessary to become successful. Make notes and highlight topics you want to remember. Each time you read it, you'll learn something new. Managing this way is not a part-time thing. Do it every day and with every employee, to the best of your ability. If you make it required reading for your assistant managers, as well, the entire management staff can actually contribute and help each other develop and improve.

You'll have successes and failures. Learn to laugh at yourself so you don't take every mistake too seriously. Simply learn from them and move on. Henry Ford once said, "Anyone who stops learning is old, whether at twenty or eighty. Anyone who keeps learning stays young."

If every business practiced sound management fundamentals, companies would rarely have to hire a manager. Entry-level positions would be the only jobs available. Every time a manager got promoted, the assistant manager would already be trained and ready to take his place. Most of the employees would be cross-trained and taught the skills needed to assume additional responsibilities, so choosing an assistant manager from that pool of top-notch employees would simply be a matter of selecting the best person for promotion. The only task left would be to interview and hire the best candidate for the job that became available. The torch of knowledge would be passed on and the cycle of training continued.

This is a learning process that will last your whole life. Make your goal to be one of always wanting to improve your management skills and passing on that knowledge to your employees. Your particular management journey will then be prosperous and one to remember. Good luck.

Notes

Notes

www.ingramcontent.com/pod-product-compliance
Lightning Source LLC
Chambersburg PA
CBHW030811180526
45163CB00003B/1240